A LITTLE PIGEON TOAD

written and illustrated by

FRED GWYNNE

Simon and Schuster Books for Young Readers
Published by Simon & Schuster Inc., New York

SIMON AND SCHUSTER
BOOKS FOR YOUNG READERS
Simon & Schuster Building
Rockefeller Center
1230 Avenue of the Americas
New York, New York 10020

Manufactured in the United States of America

10 9 8 7 6 5 4 3 2 1

Library of Congress Cataloging-in-Publication Data
Gwynne, Fred.
A little pigeon toad/by Fred Gwynne.
p. cm.
SUMMARY: Humorous text and illustrations introduce
a variety of homonyms and figures of speech.
1. English language—Homonyms—Juvenile literature.
2. Figures of speech—Juvenile literature. [1. English
language—Homonyms. 2. Figures of Speech.] I. Title.
PE1595.G77   1988 428. 1—dc19   88-11501
                                    CIP
                                    AC
ISBN 0-671-66659-2

For My Father

Mommy says

Daddy is a little pigeon toad.

Grandma says our four bears

came from Scotland.

Daddy says tennis rackets
should be taught…

…and you can teach dogs to heal.

My teacher says

I get along well with my piers.

Mommy says trees have knots…

...and flowers have pistols.

…and flowers have pistols.

Daddy says city streets

have man holes.

Mommy says

there are naval oranges.

Mommy says her coat is
a little thread bear.

Daddy knows a man who fished

for a giant hammerhead.

Daddy says Mommy

is in bed with hives.

Daddy says he wants a pool table.

After dinner Mommy and Daddy

are going to show their slides.

In Sunday School they
say when you are bad
you should do pennants.

Daddy says he pitched a tent.

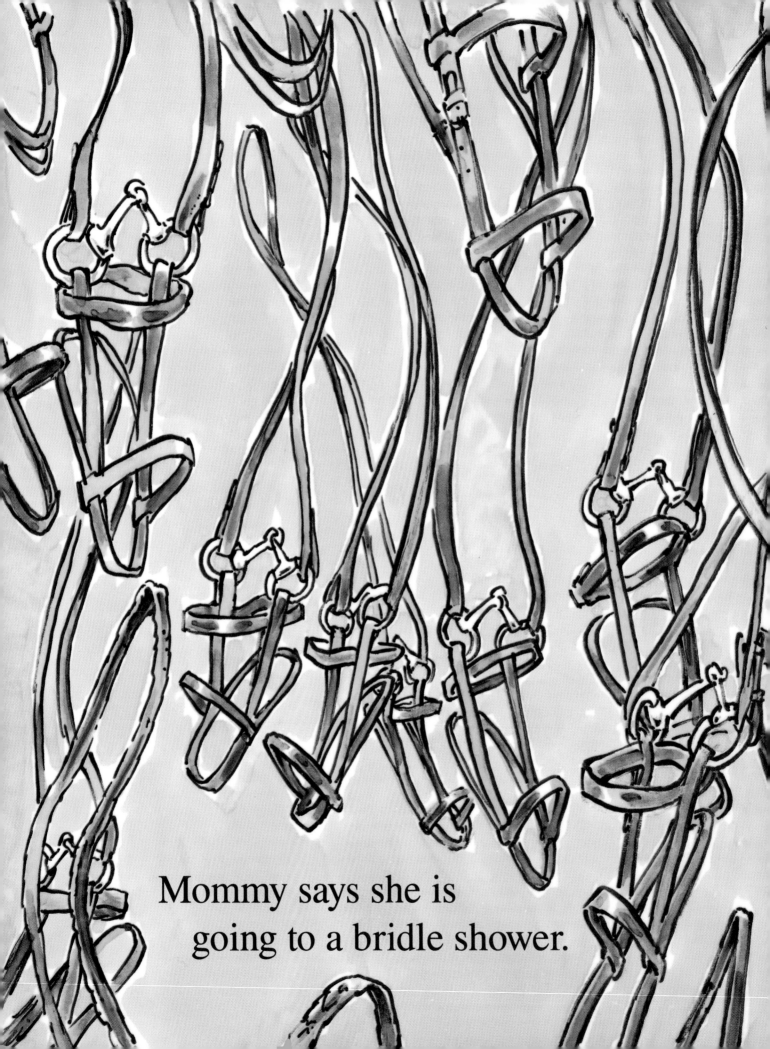

Mommy says she is
going to a bridle shower.

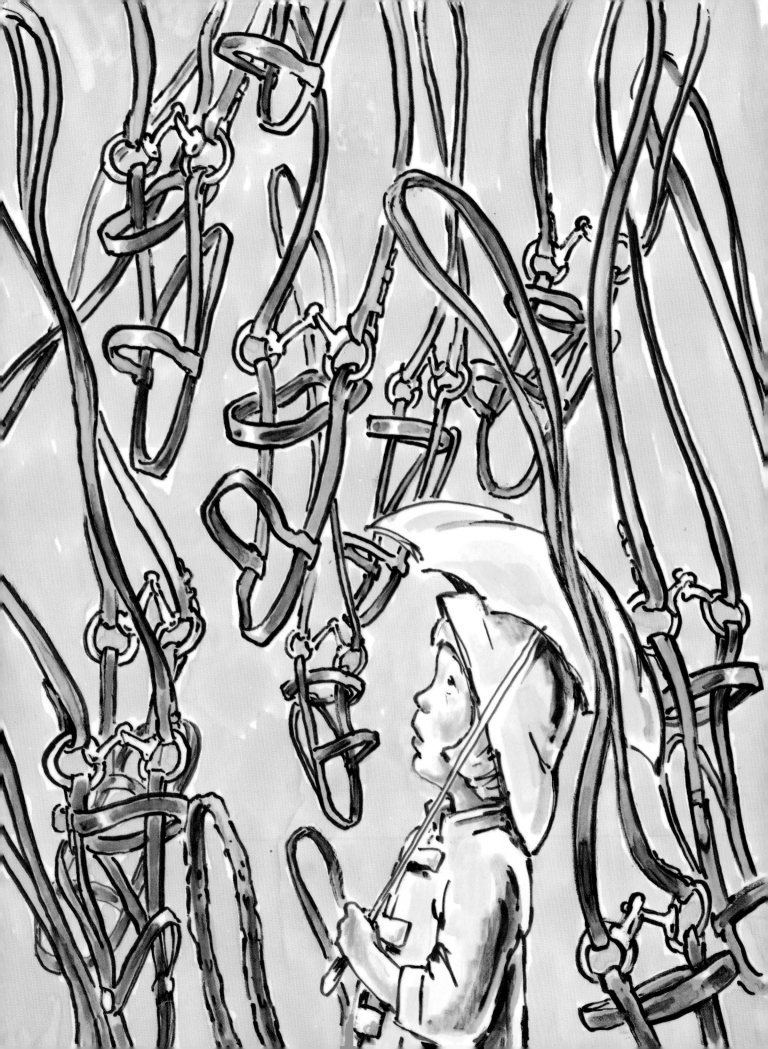

Uncle Walter says he

sews his fields…

…and lives off the land.

Daddy says I'm his air.

Daddy says there are

three feet in a yard.

Yarns like these
are hard to swallow!